the flap pamphlet series

Grammar of Passage

flap

open, read, turn

Grammar of Passage

the flap pamphlet series (No. 20)
Printed and Bound in the United Kingdom

Published by the flap series, 2020
the pamphlet series of flipped eye publishing
All Rights Reserved

Cover Design by Petraski
Series Design © flipped eye publishing, 2010

Author Photo © Anna Yarrow
First Edition
Copyright © Monika Cassel, 2020

The following poems have appeared, sometimes in slightly different forms, in these publications:

"Asparagus officinalis: Mannheim 1956." *Construction Literary Magazine*, Fall 2019.
"Schloß Porcia, Spittal, July 1941." *The Speakeasy Project Session Five Anthology*, Summer 2018
"Feeding Cake to the Storks." *Phoebe Journal* 45.1, Fall 2015.
"Arrival" *Laurel Review*, Spring 2015.
"Thrift, ca. 1947," and "Hertha Tielsch to Maria Radler, Garßen bei Celle, January 1, 1947." *Sixfold* Summer 2014.

[A few passages in "*Asparagus officinalis*: Mannheim 1956" are quotations from or references to Margot Schubert's 1946 gardening manual, *Mein Eigner Garten*, (the original is in German; translations are the author's).

Other sources include family films shot between 1937 and 1956 and family letters written between 1945 and 1950 by the author's grandmother, Hertha Tielsch, her grandfather, Albrecht Tielsch, and her great-uncle, Edgar Schröder.]

ISBN: 978-1-905233-59-5

Supported using public funding by
ARTS COUNCIL ENGLAND
LOTTERY FUNDED

For my daughters, Helen and Phoebe Harrison

Grammar of Passage

by Monika Cassel

Contents | *Grammar of Passage*

Arrival

After the noise, pulse, stink, and power of the flights, orange plastic chairs in endless Kennedy waiting halls, jabs of competing elbows, my father's cramped snores, bus from Luxembourg and then hefting luggage into a taxi, the cabby's Mannheim accent as he drags on his dangling cigarette, smell and echo of the old elevator and stairwell (granite, wood, a memory of dust), a kiss on my grandmother's cheek – high up and surprisingly soft in the face with the stern eyes, forbidding lips – white-tablecloth lunch of Kassler Rippchen und Sauerkraut on the balcony with a quick sip of mother's beer, barges puttering coal-smoke along the Rhine below, and a nap behind the rattling jalousies that admit only particles of afternoon light:

> awakening in a cool room on a down-and-terry covered horse-hair bed, sheeted lime-green, to scrutinize in the twilight the dots, cross-hatches, and triangles of the wallpaper
>> swimming like blue and grey sails in a lake of cream.

Portrait of My Grandmother's Hair in the 1940s

Dark,
brown in the color shots, rolled in waves
off her temples, the coils changing height and angle
in every film, raised, lowered,

glossy, thick as a river,
strong as the hair I try in vain to tame
on the head of my eldest daughter,

caught in the back, gathered at the nape in knots and braids,
new patterns every season:
hair any man would want to unravel.

The light silver-sepia, movement
in the start and end of her smile
as the camera captures her from behind, from the side
when she turns
to wipe a mouth, lift a baby, throw a ball, pour cognac or cocoa or tea –

we see her
from all angles, as when, bent over,
holding the hands of a child (my mother)
who is learning to walk
her hair   defines

her face

she's so pretty,
my daughter breathes
staring for the first time
at the woman she never knew
whose features and gestures we both share

and whom I, too, never knew,
or not like this: a woman with young children,
her husband still alive and behind the camera.
Here, she is someone who in the morning

(before anyone enters the frame)   might raise
her arm above her head
to twist a strand of hair,
fix a pin –

sitting at the edge of her bed an instant longer
to gaze at her husband's back
as he leans over the washstand
and then turns after rinsing his chin
to glance at her once more
before pulling a clean shirt from the wardrobe –

– she fixes the last strand
and then rises to enter
another day in a wartime
they'll keep off
                    the screen.

More than fifty years later she'll
hand their love letters to her daughter
with orders to discard them,
the man long dead, too long,

(the daughter glancing through the folded papers
one single time
as she places them in the bin)

so that no one else will ever know   the words
that passed between them.

Schloß Porcia, Spittal, July 1941

*"Weißt Du nicht, was gestern Du zu mir gesagt
bei dem kühlen Brunnenwasser?"*

– „Der Froschkönig"

The nurse has taken the children
back by boat so they can hike
from Spittal to Seeboden. They've stopped
to see the palace. Flight by flight,
she pans the courtyard's storied arches
with the camera and her architect's eye.

White limestone cut and placed to soar,
to last, to cradle a fated Spanish dynasty.
The palace rises above them as the camera lifts
and turns and falls, then she cuts
to film her husband as he climbs the staircase
which, porticoed, rises under ascending arches.

It's like her early married life, this scene –
the squares and white tower of Pisa
where a child miscarried and the nurse in hospital
brought red wine to fortify her.

*when you bleed you need to drink red things, my German roommate
said, uncorked another bottle*

The renaissance arrived four hundred years ago
in Austria, reached its height
within these palace walls. They are more Italy than Austria,
but Austria is Germany now and war is on,
though in the garden restaurant
the waitress still pours soup
from shining pitchers into low, wide bowls.

earlier, when he filmed her at dinner on the terrace, her quiet mouth like
mine, something hooded and familiar in her eyes.

As he climbs, her husband bears the camera case
on leather straps; his jacket is white. He turns
to face her as he gains the landing
and rounds the corner;
his figure fades where it is dark.

down at the pier, their children feed a pair of swans

She climbs behind him,
trains the camera across the dated coat of arms
up on the wall. Then they walk
and she films elderberries
in bloom, waters rushing
over a dam. He's in shirtsleeves now,
leans over the railing of one narrow bridge
and walks another, eyes down,
his shape receding.

my daughters far off-flowers, their roots grow, yellow asphodel.

Now we see the river from above,
the valley it has carved, strong-watered,
the road an asphalt S this place must bear.
A couple strolls below and two men cycle,
heading home down to the village
in the valley where on weekends
soldiers march their blood-red banners.

their not-yet voices hum. At night, my husband delivers babies.

In the last frame
she's stepped ahead,
films him walking in her direction

in colored glasses, shirtsleeves rolled,
his jacket on his arm. Water glides below.
He speaks and, smiling, steps out of the shade.

*will you be true to me as I am true to you? Where did you go, and
should I follow?*

Morning, East Prussia, 1942

The schoolgirl takes a packet of bread and butter
from her mother's hand as she heads off,
turns and waves at the gate.

Cut to a boy pulling a dachshund on a leash,
cut to soldiers
marching ten Russian POWs down the street.

On the street, deep-gabled houses.

Cut to the kids who play
in the dirt lane by the iron fence,
to my mother, two years old,

rubbing her eyes (she's crying),
her flowered pinafore
fastened over her sweater.

Morning now over, the school door opens
and my uncle, eager after hours of waiting,
tugs the girl as she goes by:

he will play with his cousin
in the yard with the branching trees;
she will demonstrate sums on her slate.

Cut to the airplane approaching overhead, then cut

as it flies off
over the schoolhouse. It must be German
or they'd all run for cover.

The girl is beautiful
and already knows how to flirt
with the camera. Her mother,

a beauty too, doesn't care
when people say she's too kind to the Russians
who do the forestry work, doesn't know

the years her husband will spend in captivity.

Cut to the POWs: they split kindling,
pile it round, splits tossed
into the center

of a carefully composed round stack.
Only one
looks up at the camera.

The Wehrmacht soldiers,
on the other hand,
turn, grinning, rifles at ease:

at last the man composing the wall atop the pile
looks down
to where my grandfather holds the camera

and smiles.

Bath Time, Herzogenrath (1943)

Sailing ship in the boy's hands. In the center of the frame a hand rubs a foot with a sponge. Wet, both foot and hand shine in the light which comes from behind, just so, from the window. At the head of the tub, in the dark background, another pair of hands lifts the girl's foot and does the same. Then we see the boy's face. His hair has grown dark in the past year, he's on his belly, a giant tadpole with new front legs pushing his body back and forth while his sister watches, admiring. Now he's stepped out and stands, glistening; a woman's dark head ducks into the foreground as she bends to dry him. Her combs reflect the light, which from this angle is meager.

The girl is still in the tub. She holds a small fish in her right hand, a small swan with black wings in her left. At the top of her head, her hair is tied back with a ribbon; in an earlier frame her pageboy is so short that you can see where her neck has been shaved. As hands float her back and forth she smiles at the camera and then is lifted up and out. While she is rubbed dry with a big white towel, she leans over the bath and drops the bird in so that it can swim. She prances with delight and the camera follows her feet. She turns back, looks just to the left at something or someone; her mouth opens in a happy shriek.

Night falls outside.

"We took precautions"
(1945)

The spoons are in the well,
The bread and coffee's

in the bed
nestled

against the girl
playing sick –

The sewing machine saved
by trailing the British soldier;

he toured the house
and paused down cellar

where he'd buried it under coals, left
red-faced and empty-handed.

Though it's forbidden,
some give the children gum.

We lost
our sheets and tablecloths,

white linen
the Americans used

for winter camouflage
at the house we fled.

We glean potatoes
from the farmer's field.

They made the neighbors tour
the camp just down the road:

but we weren't told
to go. So much we

strain to save;
so much kept hidden.

Thrift, ca. 1946

„Die Fahne hoch! Die Reihen stets geschlossen!"
　　　　　(Title and first line of the song "Raise the Flag,"
　　　　　co-anthem during the Third Reich, composed by Horst Wessel,
　　　　　Nazi hero and martyr, and banned in Germany after 1945)

She made me a new red dress
when the schools opened again:
pulled the old flag out from a drawer,
clipped the stitches
from the circle in the center, held it up,
shook her head
at the black spider,

"good fabric
and a pity to waste it
but there's just nothing
I can make out of this,"
spread the red rectangle
and cut the pattern;
just enough.

A lot of girls wear red
these days. At recess
boys patrol
the playground. They sing
Horst Wessel's song
as they run by,
„Die Fahne hoch!", yank up
our skirts.

Rutabagas, Potatoes, Plums (1945-7)

I haven't yet responded to your questions
about the food situation:

> I was playing hide-and-seek
> in the hedges by the roadside
> when a soldier passed and saw me.

> He gave me chocolate.

Meat we get just 150g/week
and 100 g Schmalz
but in the Russian zone, they say,
you don't get either

> school meals were always better
> in the US zone, orange cheese
> and peanut butter

Bread and grains we have enough;
we're lucky to have potatoes and rutabagas
so I think we'll get through the winter fairly well.
This week we'll cook syrup
from the sugar beets.

> The Russians came through
> and Mutti put me in bed
> with the bread and silver,
> clucked through the house,
> "Kind krank, Kind krank!"
> as if I still had typhus.

for us the ration equalization
was a dead loss

                                    She'd make porridge:
                    rye ground in the coffee mill,
                              flavored with parsley,
                                            potato.

schmalz or margarine 50g more
for adults
but 100 g less per child

                                    The big dilemma –
                    eat the potato first, or save the best
                                          for last?

so we four get 100 g less:
a dead loss.

            We were only allowed to eat the plums that fell from the tree
                        or Tante Alice would scold us. But sometimes
                                  when plums were dark and ripe

            Vati would bump into the tree as he walked by and laugh
                                        with rain of plums
                                    which we'd then gather,

                    Her stern face frowning from the window.

Hertha Tielsch to Maria Radler,
Garßen bei Celle, January 23, 1947.

I've enclosed
your handkerchief
which I am returning
to you, unfortunately
still with the stain.

I just laid it in the snow
one more time
to bleach –

Maybe that
will help.

Cutting Peat, 1947

"Unseren Torf haben wir in sehr gutem Zustand am Pfingstdienstag hereingebracht. Diese Sorge haben wir also nicht mehr. Am Sonntag Mittag der Woche deines Hierseins waren wir fertig. 6150 Stück."
– Hertha Tielsch to Maria Radler, June 12, 1947*

I.

My mother is running in the yard.
Her wooden shoes jump
on clods of grass and she swings a stick
to roll a hoop. Her brother rides the family bicycle
in loops around her. Her braids are swinging too. Then
they stop their play and gather kindling; they pull a wagon
to where their mother begins to stack the splits in a broad circle.

In his neat suit, their grandfather splits more kindling.
He's only sixty-seven but looks bent and old.

Just out of the frame,
the apple trees
have again begun to bloom.

II.

Everything turns, eventually, to a shovel's push,
the matted earth ten thousand years old,
my grandfather, forty-three, my age,
in the bog in undershirt and shorts

---

* "We brought in our peat in very good condition on Tuesday after Pentecost. So that care is behind us now. On Sunday noon of the week of your visit here we were done. 6150 pieces."

– Hertha Tielsch to Maria Radler, June 12, 1947

and not his chemist's suit.
Ankle-deep in mud, he works:
the tool handles crooked, made perhaps
from saplings or from branches,

spade and then the forked hoe,
pole-handled bucket, wheelbarrow.
My grandfather's back arches, bends, and bends again;
the turf is rich and black and falls into the pit.

And yet this is a day they choose to document: what glint
the camera gives the water falling,
the hoe while mixing all into the rich and bitter dough
they'll make the bricks with in the field.

The wheelbarrow must be filled, and filled again
and pushed, all full of wet and heavy earth,
to where they'll dry it. Below, the dark sticks
like plaster to everything it touches.

III.

My grandmother wears a peasant blouse hand-edged with blanket stitch,
the halter dress with checkered pockets she wore in a restaurant on vaca-
tion just five years ago. A kerchief, mud-splattered, covers up her hair.
She wears her watch. Will mud jam up the works? Will marking time
make her work light?

> She takes a heavy shovel
> of peat and smoothes it
> in the mold; she lifts
> the wood and metal frame,
> sets it down again just
> one step back and tamps
> it once with her left
> foot. She lifts the shovel

again. Now she begins a
new row; five more wet
bricks lie upon the open
field. Minute by minute more
lumps gleam in columns and
rows. She lifts and fills
the frame and lifts again.
Like a second hand's ticking
the bricks trace her slow
track across the meadow as
she punches out one more
row. Now half the field
is black with soldiers' lines
of soft wet mud drying
slowly in May's light sun.

IV

Their bicycles rest against the trunk behind them
and they have spread a broad-striped cloth.
She lies propped on her elbow,
eats from a shallow metal dish. We see her watch again
but cannot read the time. Her face is almost blank
as she spoons porridge that would be grey
even if this film were shot in color.

The camera cuts. Now the dishes lie clean
and empty, neat, upon the cloth. She has already washed them.

We see her lying
as if asleep,
her face still flecked with mud.

The camera cuts again, and he is lying on the blanket now.
His face reflects the light that falls

between the branches
of the tree. He, too, has closed his eyes.

They rest. They have passed the camera back and forth to show us this.

V

They do not film the work that afternoon, but on it goes:
Their future uncertain, broken world all around them
as the thousand-year-old earth, a viscous muck, is lifted, lifted, packed.

It dries on one side,
then each brick is turned;
They labor on.

VI

She must have ridden ahead
to tell the children they were coming home
so she could film his great return
that afternoon, weaving bicycle and towed wheelbarrow
through the lane of flowering apple trees
their blossoms heavy and swaying in the wind,
so bright in the late sunlight of the day.

His son has ridden out to greet him and now pedals behind
while his daughter, almost unseen,
skips along beneath the blossoms.
He has ridden past the camera
and steers around the house into the unlit woodshed.
He is wearing a white shirt now,
it is rolled up to his elbows and looks clean.

VII

When the field is filled with dark shapes
when the local farmer comes with tractor, wagon, and gas ration
when the whole family goes to the bog to help
when the girl with braids drops bricks into a basket
when her braids swing when she steps to lift and to refill it
when she is seven
when you know it is a hunger year and she owns only two dresses
when the refugees billeted in the house work beside her: a schoolteacher,
       his wife and his daughter
when your uncle is a surly-looking boy in glasses
when the children's grandfather takes the handle of a basket, and his
       daughter takes the other
when you see from the way her left arm stretches out to balance the load
       that it is heavy
when the pile of bricks in the wagon grows ever higher
when the kitchen is warm and there are bricks for stoves and for wash water
when the large house is hard to heat but houses seventeen people
when the farmer drives the tractor
when your grandfather holds the camera as he sits ahead of the driver,
       perhaps on the engine chassis
when the farmer grins into the camera in a startling close-up, all cap and
       crooked teeth
when the others ride atop the high peat pile; this is the earth they have
       inherited
when the camera bounces with the bump of the tractor on the roads
when you look at the map and calculate how close the camp was

when in the final scene you see trees as the tractor rattles off on the rutted
       road with empty wagon
when the children run behind it
when you must imagine how it sounded because the film is silent

when the peat is rich but the field looks faded
when your grandmother writes letters about how tired she is

when you read letters in which she despairs about her future
when you read letters in which she despairs about her country
when you ask as you read what she means
when you wonder what peat smells like when it burns
when you know how silent many questions made her
when the film is sometimes overexposed
when you never see these scenes in color
when your daughters' smiles remind you of her mouth when it was
        younger
when you remember from one childhood visit how the heath looks
        abloom
when you look again into the faces as if into eddies in a river

Asparagus officinalis: **Mannheim, 1956**
(*Mein Eigner Garten* 202-6)

> "*Bis Johanni nicht vergessen,*
> *Sieben Wochen Spargel essen.*"
> (Asparagus Menu, Restaurant Reichskrone, Heidelberg 2014)

I.

My mother holds the knife and trowel up for the camera.
Bell skirt, ponytail, sixteen,
her chiffon scarf a soft wish
to be in this new world.

She walks the beds.
Her brother's eating raspberries by the hedge.

II.

Egyptians and Romans, the book says:
asparagus came up the Rhine
with Caesar's legions and the eagle standard.

French poets and philosophers debated recipes
for centuries – "But the gardener doesn't care
whether we eat it with our fingers at table
or spear it with our forks,

or cut off all the heads for our own plate
in delicious disregard for the feelings of others;
he contents himself with his asparagus cutter
and, of course, his skillful hands."

III.

Along the rows

they wait underground,
rising to the surface

like the unexploded ordnance from the war
revealed each spring
when farmers plow their fields
or children run on forest paths.

There is rubble still uncleared,
pockmarked façades of houses,
the streets and buildings grey all year
with smokestack soot and winter's coal-dust

stories hushed of who was taken
and what exactly happened on the front,
the iron pins now stashed in desk drawers

uniforms still hanging
at the back of some old wardrobes.

IV.

Not Caesar's legions now:
The army down the road
is from across the ocean.

V.

The garden book advises us
on how to dig the trenches,
their proper orientation to the winds,
the placement of the roots at planting

("This first asparagus shoot must be protected like a raw egg
and handled delicately, because the realization
of all of our future asparagus joys
is dependent on its welfare"),

the three-year cycle before first harvest,
and when to spread manure, potash, phosphate
after harvest's done.

It teaches us to keep the earthen mounds well-heaped
for shoots that must not see the sun, well-covered.

VI.

My mother has weeded the beds
for five years now. She's cut her childhood braids.
What joy
knows it is dependent on her welfare?

VII.

This delicate,
wholesome vegetable.

VIII.

Not a stalk has burst
full-fledged, pale shoots all; never to green
in springtime light, they grow below
like all the buried stories

and don't burst up unbidden
as long as watchful eyes look every day.
The crop is good,
the garden nicely tended.

IX.

She digs and cuts and covers,
one stalk, and then another.

Grammar of Passage

(train through south Germany, 2014)

Wheat fields, church spires and trees in quick succession;
red-tiled roofs, hills, greenhouses, and fields again;
a man-made lake, three rivers, stone lace
of one great town's cathedral tower;
a windmill, solitary upon a hill.

The train's wheels whine and rumble dark
past a brewery, past warehouses piled
like loaves of bread along the tracks:
We're speeding towards, away, unknown –
each second we articulate, it changes.

We're *here* and *here* and *here*,
almost a note of interrogation
everywhere and in between
the arid mountains of my home
and these ancestral fields of green,
a sentence still unfolding that won't ever let me go –

How everything's an elegy,
even as my children walk with me along the platform,
my daughter, as we walk the train cars, stops me for a quick embrace
just as I see a bicycle that's parked beside the corn;
a man nearby in red, bent over, works his field.

Everything's punctuation, a *there* and *there* and *there*,
the apple trees arrayed across that hill,
the now now now of the pigeons who strut the city platform
an endless present, heads a-bobbing as they range:
They're here, they change.

Feeding Cake to the Storks

Die Felder sind so braun.
       They are brown and olive-green,
as if they had forgotten singing
and the soft touch of wheat
as it murmurs among the poppies and cornflowers in May.

I look from platform to track
and dream your coat,
snapping past concrete-ringed houses,
encased in ice
and floating across frozen fields.

I see sunflowers from the train
and heat rises from them; I dream
scarlet rashes of weeds in your corn.
When I dream your coat and flowers in winter
I am Ruth, making my way through foreign avenues
laced with dark coffee,
made of thick bread.

I will displace you;
I have mixed the seasons
in our dreams and this dry platform
as it leads another train below,
from field to city –

       – I can't tell you.
In the East lie old family estates:
Storks nest in their archives, sing
on my grandparents' graves;
I will travel and throw crumbs behind me to mark my way.